7 Seconds to Success

Gary Coffey
Bob Phillips

HARVEST HOUSE PUBLISHERS
EUGENE, OREGON

Cover by Dugan Design Group, Bloomington, Minnesota

7 SECONDS TO SUCCESS
Copyright © 2010 by Gary Coffey and Bob Phillips
Published 2012 by Harvest House Publishers
Eugene, Oregon 97402
www.harvesthousepublishers.com

Library of Congress Cataloging-in-Publication Data

Coffey, Gary, 1943–
   7 seconds to success / Gary Coffey and Bob Phillips.
      p. cm.
   ISBN 978-0-7369-4618-6 (pbk.)
   ISBN 978-0-7369-4619-3 (eBook)
   1. Interpersonal communication. I. Phillips, Bob, 1940– . II. Title.
BF637.C45C625 2012
650.1'3—dc23   2011048730

Printed in the United States of America

12 13 14 15 16 17 18 19 20 / BP-KBD / 10 9 8 7 6 5 4 3 2 1

To my good friend
Rich "Cotton" Buhler,
1946–2012.
Without his encouragement and
inspiration this book
wouldn't have been written.

Gary Coffey

Acknowledgments

We would like to thank our family and friends for encouraging us to write this book.

We could not have accomplished this work without God giving us the time and resources to finish.

And I (Gary) would like to give a special thanks to John Slevcove for the use of his cabin at Hume Lake, California—a very special place to think and write.

Contents

· · · · · · · · · · · · · · ·

1

The Beginning

There was a smile on Scott's face when he sat down in the leather chair. He nodded slightly as he thought about his week. One of his escrows was closing on Monday, and two more were due to close on Friday. He had three new listings coming up by the end of next week. He knew Sarah would be excited at the good news.

His thoughts were interrupted by engine noise. He glanced out the living room window and saw a Dodge Caravan park in front of the house. A tall, thin man and a woman, probably his wife, emerged from the pristine white van. The woman opened the sliding door, and two children got out.

Scott watched as the couple stood in front of the Open House sign. They talked and pointed to various things in the neighborhood. He could see they were serious and a little hesitant. As they came down the walk toward the front door, he noticed that the husband's walk was a little tentative, while the woman was walking casually. Quickly Scott asked two important questions: *Up or down? Left or right?* Then he decided, *This couple looks like a Thinker and a Toucher.* He waited until the doorbell rang before he got up.

"Good afternoon, folks," Scott said with a big smile after he opened the door. "My name is Scott McFadden. Welcome to the open house." He held out his hand, and they all exchanged handshakes.

"Hi! My name is Becky. This is my husband, Alan, and our two kids, Joey and Beth."

Observing that the husband's eyes shied away from a direct look and he had a reserved sort of smile, Scott silently confirmed, *He* is *a Thinker.* Noticing the husband was looking around, Scott quickly handed him a brochure before turning to the wife. "Shall we get started in the kitchen?" he asked.

The wife held the hand of one of the children while the husband held the other child's hand.

"Where are you folks from?" Scott asked.

"We're from Simi Valley," replied the wife.

"That's a great area. I have friends who live near the Simi Valley Mall."

"Oh, that's close by where we live!" Becky said with a big smile.

When they moved toward the living room, Scott asked, "What professions are you in?"

"I'm a schoolteacher, and my husband is an engineer."

"How many bedrooms are you looking for?"

The husband finally spoke. "We're looking for four bedrooms. I want to turn one of them into an office."

"Do you have a particular price range?"

Alan was quick to respond. "We can't go any higher than $500,000."

Scott smiled politely. "Well, this home is a five bedroom with three baths. It's on the market for $575,000." He sensed their disappointment. "However, if you step into the dining room with me, I can show you a few homes in this neighborhood with four bedrooms in your price range."

For the next ten minutes Scott shared the various features of the prospective homes. He then gave the couple printouts on the details of the houses.

"I suggest you drive by and see if any of them appeal to you." Scott noticed the husband's body relaxed a little.

"Thank you so much for all of your suggestions and help," Becky said.

"I appreciate your honesty," Alan added. "At the last open house we visited, the salesperson really put pressure on us to buy. We don't have time to look at these other homes today, but we'd like to work with you. Do you have time tomorrow?"

Scott quickly checked his appointment book and asked how one o'clock sounded. After Becky nodded, Scott handed her his business card. "We can meet at my office. It's close by." He gave directions and then walked them to the door. "Thank you for stopping by. It was sure nice meeting you." After shutting the door, Scott walked to the window and watched as the couple buckled their children into the rear seats of the Dodge Caravan, got into the front seats, and then drove off. He smiled. Then his thoughts turned back to how he'd learned to read people so well.

———

Scott was excited when he graduated from college. He was so ready to enter the workforce. But then the economic downturn hit. The only job he could get was working as a salesclerk in the Electronics Department at Sears—a far cry from what he'd hoped for as a business major in school. He'd set his sights on the great American dream, but it was becoming more like a nightmare. He and his wife, Sarah, both worked to make ends meet. They wanted to move out of their small apartment and buy their own place someday.

Scott finally decided to take a real estate course in the evenings. He hoped it would be the avenue for them to get ahead. But that road was turning into a dead-end street. He'd been smart enough to keep his job at Sears, so he worked real estate in his off hours and on weekends.

This was his third open house, and few people were showing up. He was bored and discouraged as he sat in the quiet house. Slowly he got up and looked out the living room window. The street was empty. He nervously tucked his sport shirt into his Dockers and adjusted his belt. He rubbed his fingers through his blond hair and let out a long sigh. *I wonder if all real estate people experience this?* he thought. Then he was reminded what his father had told him before he passed away. "Son, remember what Thomas Edison said. 'I never allow myself to become discouraged under any circumstances...The three great essentials to achieve anything worthwhile are first, hard work; second, stick-to-itiveness; third, common sense.' "

Scott let out another sigh. To kill some of the wait time, he opened the paper he'd purchased that morning. To get his mind off no one coming to his open house, he even resorted to reading the advertisements. That's when he saw it.

"That's the seminar for me!" Scott said out loud. "I only wish I could afford to go." He ran his fingers through his hair again and let out another long sigh. He put down the paper and stared out the window at the still-empty street. *There has to be a better way to get ahead,* he decided.

Insight

· · · · · · · · · · · · ·

*I never allow myself to become
discouraged under any circumstances...
The three great essentials to achieve
anything worthwhile are first, hard work;
second, stick-to-itiveness;
third, common sense.*

THOMAS EDISON

2

The Encounter

Scott, do you remember that newspaper ad you showed me a couple weeks ago?" Sarah asked.

"What ad?"

"The one about the 'Seven Seconds to Success' seminar."

"Yes. It was held last week in Anaheim near Disneyland. I sure wish I could've gone. What about it?"

"I was watching the news on TV before you came home. One story said that Gordon Paddock is going to do a book signing at the Barnes & Noble Bookstore. That's only two miles away. You should go! It's tonight at eight."

"I'm not even sure we have enough money to buy his book," Scott muttered.

"You should go anyway. Maybe you could meet him."

"And then what? Ask him if he will give me a free ticket to his next seminar?"

"Who knows what might happen, Scott," Sarah said. "My father always told me that when opportunity knocks, make sure you go to the door."

"Well, I don't hear any knocking."

"Dad also said that sometimes we must make our own opportunities. What do you have to lose, Scott? Why not go?" Sarah watched him. She knew he was deep in thought.

~~~

When Scott arrived at Barnes & Noble, the parking lot was full. *It looks like I'm not the only person who wants to meet Gordon Paddock.* He finally found a parking spot a block and a half from the store. He got out of his car and headed down the sidewalk. He only got a few feet when he stopped and shook his head. *What am I doing here? There's no way this guy is going to help me.* Scott turned back to his car, and then his father's words about Edison flashed into his mind again. "The three great essentials to achieve anything worthwhile are first, hard work; second, stick-to-itiveness; third, common sense." He hesitated for a moment and then let out a sigh. He turned and headed to the bookstore.

The place was packed when he entered. Scott worked his way to the back where he could glimpse Gordon Paddock. He was sitting at a desk autographing books for people who were obviously very excited. Scott could see that the man's chalk-striped blue suit was expensive and fit the businessman's squared shoulders perfectly. Gordon was a tall man, probably in his late fifties, who looked quite distinguished with his salt-and-pepper-colored hair.

Scott watched as Paddock smiled and gave a personal greeting to each person he signed a book for. He didn't seem to tire of being polite, even though he must have been signing books for forty-five minutes or more. Scott didn't know what to do other than observe the author, whose emerald eyes graciously responded to the strangers. *I can see why people are attracted to him,* Scott thought. As the crowd grew smaller, Scott noticed that Paddock looked at him several times and smiled.

Finally the last person received his autographed book. Paddock put the cap on an expensive Mont Blanc pen and slipped it into his coat pocket. He leaned back in his chair and looked at Scott.

Paddock's green eyes locked on Scott's powder-blue ones. There was an ever-so-slight smile on the author's lips. He stood up, revealing his six-foot-three frame, and walked toward Scott.

Scott felt a twinge of nervousness.

"My name is Gordon Paddock. What's yours?" the man said as he stuck out his hand and gave a warm smile that enveloped Scott.

Scott smiled back. "I'm Scott MacFadden." Scott's right hand was encased in a strong, firm handshake. It was the kind that got your attention and could be felt even after the person let go.

"Nice to meet you, Scott. I'm a little thirsty after all this talking. Would you like to join me for a cup of coffee next door at Starbucks? I'm buying."

The invitation was given sincerely and openly, so Scott felt comfortable accepting. Paddock had a commanding yet pleasant presence.

After checking in with the bookstore manager, Gordon told Scott he was ready. The two men headed next door. Entering Starbucks, they ordered. When they received their drinks, they found a table. After sitting down and a few introductory pleasantries, Paddock got straight to the point. "I noticed you standing and watching the book signing for quite a period of time. Is there some way I can help you?"

Scott hesitated for a moment and then got up his courage. "I saw your ad in the paper the other day—the one about your 'Seven Seconds to Success' seminar. I wanted to go, but funds have been tight for my wife and me since college."

There was a gentle smile on Gordon's lips, but he remained quiet.

Scott continued. For half an hour or so he shared his struggle with getting ahead and his discouragement in real estate. Paddock's eyes and mind seemed to absorb everything about Scott. *It's a little unnerving on one hand, but a little freeing on the other,* Scott decided.

"Thank you for being candid and honest," Paddock responded when Scott wound down. "You remind me of someone from my past." He glanced at his watch. "I've just noticed the time. My wife will be expecting me. I'm sorry I don't have time to talk further tonight. I live outside of Palm Desert in the mountains. It's about a two-hour drive, so I need to get on the road."

Paddock and Scott rose at the same time.

"Do you mind if I ask you a question, Scott?" Paddock asked as they headed to the door.

"No, of course not."

"Would you be open to coming to my ranch and talking more on this subject? Say next Saturday around one o'clock? If you aren't working, of course."

Scott took a startled, quick breath. "That would be awesome! Are you sure you don't mind?"

Paddock smiled warmly. "I told you. You remind me of someone I once knew. I'd like to help you." He took his pen out of his pocket, along with a piece of paper. He wrote down the directions to his home and his phone number.

"When you get to the intersection of highways 74 and 371, look for the signs to Paddock Ranch. It's just a short distance from there, on the right side of the road."

"Thank you, Mr. Paddock! I'm so excited about this opportunity!"

"I'll look forward to our time together," Paddock affirmed.

They said their goodbyes and went their separate ways. Scott was grinning. He couldn't wait to tell Sarah the good news.

Insights

· · · · · · · · · · · · · ·

*When opportunity knocks, make sure you
go to the door. However, sometimes we must
make our own opportunities.*

———

*Important people will help you if
you are really serious.*

3

The Ranch

Scott was full of anticipation when he reached Palm Desert and turned onto highway 74. The high desert soon gave way to large rocky areas. It wasn't long before he could see some pines. Soon he rolled down his windows to breathe in the cool, fresh mountain air. As he approached the junction of Highway 371, he saw the sign for Paddock Ranch with an arrow pointing the way. Within minutes he was turning down a spacious drive lined with white wooden fences. He could see large pastures with sleek quarter horses grazing on the rolling green grass. It was spectacular. Scott couldn't believe the difference between Palm Desert and Paddock Ranch.

In the distance he could see Gordon Paddock's home. It was a sprawling log cabin in the style of the 1800s. It had a base of rockwork and massive log posts that held up a large, covered porch. Huge windows overlooked the lawn, a small lake, and the nearby pastures. It was absolutely breathtaking.

As Scott parked, the front door opened. Out stepped Gordon Paddock dressed in jeans, tooled-leather cowboy boots, cowboy shirt, and a leather belt with a large silver buckle. He looked like John Wayne as he sauntered over to greet him.

Gordon produced a beaming smile. "Welcome to Paddock Ranch! I hope your trip wasn't too long."

Scott reached out and shook Paddock's hand. "The drive was great. You sure have a wonderful place," he said as they turned and walked toward the house.

A beautiful woman, also wearing jeans, boots, and a western shirt, appeared and stood on the porch. Her auburn hair shone in the bright sunlight.

As they approached the porch, Gordon did the introductions. "Scott, I'd like you to meet my wife, Cody. She's the best thing that's ever happened to me!"

"Pleased to meet you, Mrs. Paddock," Scott said.

"I'm so glad to meet you, Scott. Please come in," she invited with a gracious smile and firm handshake.

Scott was impressed.

After a brief tour of the house, Gordon and Scott went out to the porch. A gentle breeze wafted by as they settled in the shade.

"Scott, how would you like to learn what 'Seven Seconds to Success' is all about?" Gordon asked.

"That would be awesome, Mr. Paddock."

"Please call me Gordon."

"I'll try, but I'm not sure how comfortable I feel about it."

"I think you'll do just fine," Gordon said with a little smile. He continued. "Let me lay the foundation for the 'Seven Seconds to Success.' It comes from the concept of 'reading' people. When you first meet a customer, you need to quickly determine what his or her body language is conveying. That only takes a few seconds. Next is recognizing what social style group the person falls into. The third is determining how to relate and respond to that particular social style."

"You can do all that in just seven seconds?"

"Yes—with a little practice. When you're able to do that, you can more effectively meet your customers' needs. When their needs are addressed, they're more likely to do business with you—and tell other people how much they enjoyed working with you. And when more people do business with you, your income rises. It's the law of sowing. 'Whatever you sow, you shall also reap or harvest.'"

"That makes a lot of sense."

"Actually, it's not a new concept. And there's another one that goes with it. It's commonly called the Golden Rule: 'Do to others what you would have them do to you.'"

After Cody brought out some ice tea, they all chatted for a few minutes about the beautiful day. Then she excused herself and went into the house.

"Scott, are you up for some homework...a little assignment?" Gordon asked.

"Of course! What do suggest?"

Gordon smiled at Scott's enthusiasm. "Isn't the South Coast Plaza Shopping Center near where you live?"

"Yes, it is."

"Well, here is the first of several assignments I'd like to give you. I want you to spend a couple of hours at the South Coast Plaza watching people."

"Watching people?"

"Right. That's the first step in learning how to read body language. I want you to take a notebook and pen so you can jot down what you see people doing. Then you'll report back to me what you noticed about how people walk and talk. I want you to look at their posture, their eye contact, and their speech content, including their tone of voice. Along with those things, observe their body gestures, their reactions to others, their responses under stress, and their general facial expressions."

"That's quite an assignment."

"Maybe, but I don't think it will be as hard as you might think. Remember, I want you to make *general* observations of people's behavior. I want you to discover how to quickly make educated decisions about what their body language conveys."

"I'll do my best."

"I'm sure you will, Scott. I believe it was Thomas Fuller who said, 'The real difference between men is energy. A strong will, a settled purpose, an invincible determination can accomplish almost anything; and in this lies the distinction between great men and little men.' "

Scott sat quietly, processing what Gordon shared. Gordon was silent too.

Scott sensed Gordon was taking advantage of the silence in some way, but he wasn't sure how.

And then Gordon spoke again. "Scott, the bottom line in life is that people do what they really want to do. If you're serious, you'll put forth the effort necessary, using whatever means possible to reach your goal or objective. It all depends on what it is worth to you."

Scott nodded. "I know this is worth it to me. I appreciate this opportunity to learn from you."

"Good!" With a broad smile, Gordon said, "Now, it's time for you to put action to your thoughts. I remember a quote from Jawaharlal Nehru, a prime minister of India: 'People avoid action. Often because they are afraid of the consequences, for action means risk and danger. Danger seems terrible from a distance; it is not so bad if you have a close look at it. And often it is a pleasant companion, adding to the zest and delight of life.' You see, Scott, the most drastic and usually the most effective remedy for fear is direct action."

Scott was captivated by Gordon's extensive knowledge and powerful confidence. It was infectious.

Gordon and Scott rose as Gordon reached out and shook Scott's hand. "I'll see you next weekend, okay? At one o'clock? I'll be looking forward to hearing what you've learned."

"Thank you for your time. I'm excited too." Scott smiled, turned, and headed to his car. He got in, started the engine, and put the car in gear. He glanced over and waved at Gordon just before heading down the drive. During the ride home, he didn't turn on the radio. Instead he kept replaying his conversation with Gordon and enjoying the positive feelings coursing through him.

Insights

· · · · · · · · · · · · ·

Truly great people are gracious.

—⁓—

The real difference between men is energy. A strong will, a settled purpose, an invincible determination can accomplish almost anything; and in this lies the distinction between great men and little men.

THOMAS FULLER

—⁓—

In everything, do to others what you would have them do to you.

JESUS, MATTHEW 7:12

4

The Assignment

Scott arrived at the ranch just before one o'clock. A rare afternoon desert thunder shower had just ended. The sun was peeking through the clouds, creating wonderful shadows in the hills and valleys. He noticed several quarter horses racing each other in one of the lush pastures. He could still see the change of color on their backs due to the rain. *They seem almost as happy to be here as I am,* he decided.

Gordon was sitting on the porch reading when Scott drove up. He watched as Scott parked, got out, and walked over to the house. Gordon stood up and held out his hand. "Good afternoon, Scott!" Gordon said before offering his winning smile.

Doesn't this guy ever have a bad day? Scott wondered as they shook hands and sat down.

"What a beautiful day to sit under the cover of a porch and read a good book," Gordon commented.

"What are you reading?"

"Have you heard of Ken Blanchard?"

"Isn't he the guy who wrote *The One Minute Manager*?"

"That's right. He wrote it with Spencer Johnson. I'm reading the book he wrote with Phil Hodges called *Lead Like Jesus*. It's about servant leadership. I think it's quite insightful and very practical. I'm still learning how to be that kind of leader." Gordon smiled and then got down to business. "Now, bring me up to speed on your assignment. How did it go?"

Scott could easily tell that Paddock was a man of action who moved quickly to the bottom line—but in a very gracious manner.

"Wow! I'm not really sure where to begin. I had quite a time. It was fun watching people and their behavior."

"Did you learn anything about how people walked?"

"That was interesting. They seemed to be either in a hurry so they walked fast or they walked slow and somewhat casually. Some of the fast walkers seemed a little preoccupied or maybe even a little angry. On the other hand, some of the slow walkers seemed hesitant or even a little depressed. Of course, a lot of their slowness was because they were probably window shopping."

"That's a good start. You can gain insights about people by the way they walk."

"I also listened to people talking to each other. Some were quite loud and didn't seem to care if anyone heard them or not. It was like they were lost in their own world and weren't paying attention to the people around them. I even got the impression from some people talking on their cell phones that they wanted to have the people around them listen. It was like they were trying to make some kind of impression. It was kind of weird."

"You know, Scott, I've had that thought before too."

"Still, there were quite a few people who talked quietly. And there were those who weren't saying anything to their friends. They just listened."

"Why do you think they did that?"

"I'm not sure. It might be that they were just quiet types. Or maybe they couldn't get a word in edgewise with their talkative friends."

Gordon laughed deep and hearty.

"I also noticed that the posture of some people was rigid, and they looked uptight. Then there were those who looked really relaxed."

"What did that indicate to you?"

"The rigid ones seemed like they were having a bad day. The others looked like they didn't have a care in the world."

"What if a rigid person came to your open house? How would you respond?"

"Hmmm. I haven't considered that. I guess I'd act a little more businesslike rather than casual. I don't think he'd appreciate a happy-go-lucky salesman slapping him on the back."

"Sounds like you're beginning to see the importance of reading body language. That's the first part of the 'Seven Seconds to Success.' "

"I also noticed that some people looked people directly in the eye while others did not. The direct-eye contact people seemed more confident...or at least more interested. I couldn't really tell what the indirect eye contact people were thinking. I wasn't sure if they were shy, hesitant, or just didn't want to talk to the people they were with."

"In some countries, it's considered disrespectful if someone looks you directly in the eye. But in the United States, people appreciate some eye contact rather than avoidance. Eye contact often carries the message that you are interested in the other person and what he or she is saying."

Scott thought, *That's what Gordon does with me.* He said aloud, "I also noticed that some people only talked about facts, details, and fine points. The other ones seemed to primarily express emotions."

"You're right. There are fact-oriented people and feeling-oriented people. It sounds like you were really into this project."

"It got quite interesting after about an hour. It was fun to identify outgoing people who seemed to have many body gestures. I don't think they would be able to talk if someone tied their hands down. There were also those with few body gestures. They seemed quite restrained."

"Did you run across any people you would call uptight?"

"Yes, there were some who seemed angry. Their facial expressions were definitely negative. They looked very stressed. I could imagine them speaking harshly and sarcastically with the clerks in the stores. And some people looked fearful. It made me wonder what was going on in their lives."

Gordon's emerald eyes twinkled. "You know, Scott, it's easy to get into our own little world and only think about our own needs, stresses, and pressures. When we are fearful or angry about some circumstance, it seems to short-circuit our ability to relate positively to others. When other people pick up on our negative body language, they have a tendency to withdraw from us. Who would want to spend time or money with someone who didn't seem to care about them or their needs?"

"I see what you mean."

"Remember the Golden Rule? Do to others what you would have them to do to you."

Scott nodded.

"Scott, there are three basic factors in communication. The first is 'the content.' This is about 7 percent of communication. These are the actual words spoken. They can be positive words or negative words. The second is called 'tone of voice.' This makes up 38 percent of communication. It involves speaking in a harsh or soft manner. It also includes where you place the emphasis on the words. This emphasis gives away the true message being conveyed. The last is 'nonverbal behavior.' This comprises 55 percent of communication. It's the look in our eyes. It's how we stand and sit. It's how we walk and talk. It's our facial expressions, our postures, and our hand and arm movements."

"Sounds complicated."

"Not really. We learn to read people at an early age. Young children will feel comfortable or uncomfortable around an adult just by the way they are spoken to or treated. An angry look can cause children to cry and be fearful."

"That's true."

"It's easy to get into sloppy habits when it comes to dealing with customers, clients, and prospects. We need to become more alert in reading the people we meet. Lord Chesterfield said, 'Look in the face of the person to whom you are speaking if you wish to know his real sentiments, for he can command his words more easily than his countenance.'"

"I need to practice watching the nonverbal behavior of others more. I find I'm so introspective sometimes that I'm not aware of what's going on with people. I'm often wondering how people are responding to what I'm saying or doing."

"Scott, we'd worry less about what others think of us if we realized how seldom they do."

Scott laughed. "You got that right."

"In the area of social interaction with people, what do you think is more important—the motivation behind behavior or the actual behavior?" Paddock watched as Scott struggled with the question.

"Well, I guess it would be the motivation behind the actual behavior," Scott finally said.

"Most people would agree with you, Scott. But let me suggest that no one can really know someone else's motivation. All we see is people's behavior... their actions. When it comes to our own behavior, we judge ourselves by our motivations. When it comes to other people's behavior, we judge by their actions and words."

Scott took a minute to think. "You're right, Gordon. I do evaluate and judge people by their words and behavior. I haven't given this idea much thought."

"Let's focus on a related topic. There are four general 'social style' groups. I call them 'the Thinker,' 'the Teller,' 'the Toucher,' and 'the Talker.' After you learn to read body language, it becomes important to recognize the social style of an individual as soon as possible. This helps us know the best way to respond to him or her."

"This is becoming a little too complicated..."

Paddock noticed Scott's hesitation. "Hang with me for a minute, Scott. This will make sense in a minute. When I talk about Thinkers, I'm speaking about people like Albert Einstein or Sherlock Holmes. When it comes to United States' presidents, it would be someone like Woodrow Wilson. Or you can think of the character Spock from the old *Star Trek* series or William Shakespeare. If you read the Bible, it would be the Gospel writer Luke."

A picture of "a Thinker" formed in Scott's mind.

"I have another assignment for you. I'd like you to spend the next two weeks looking for Thinker social styles. Try to identify what they value and what annoys them. Look for their positives, or strengths, and their negatives, or weaknesses. See if you can determine how they generally respond to life. List their behaviors in the workplace and how they respond to family and friends. Also, see if you can discover what motivates them and how they make decisions."

"Wow, that's a lot to look for," Scott said, a bit overwhelmed.

"Well, let me ask you a question, Scott. Are there any Thinker types among your relatives or the people you work with?"

Scott thought for a minute and then smiled.

"By the look on your face, you must have thought of someone."

"It's a coworker at Sears. He's a real analytical type of person. You know, the nitpicky, overly organized kind. The guys at work refer to him as Mr. Perfectionist."

"I think you have a place to start. By the way, why don't you bring Sarah with you next time you come to the ranch? I'd love to meet her, and so would Cody. Cody even mentioned they could go shopping in Palm Desert while we talk—if your wife is interested."

"I'll ask her," Scott answered. "I'm sure she'd like to come. Thanks, Gordon."

"I'll see you in a couple of weeks then," Gordon said as they stood and shook hands.

Insight

· · · · · · · · · · · ·

When it comes to our own behavior,
we judge ourselves by our motivations.
When it comes to other people's behavior,
we judge them by their actions and words.

5

The Thinker

Scott was excited and yet a little apprehensive as he drove down the fence-lined drive to the ranch. He was enthusiastic because Sarah was going to meet Gordon and Cody. He was apprehensive because he wanted to please Gordon Paddock. He wanted to prove that he was really serious about getting ahead. He was so grateful for this opportunity to be mentored by such an obviously successful and personable man.

Sarah was staring out the window, overwhelmed by the beauty of the pastures and grazing horses.

"Scott, you told me it was beautiful, but this is breathtaking."

As they rounded the corner and could see the little lake in front of the log home, Sarah took a deep breath. "You've got to be kidding! This is like a scene in a storybook."

As they neared the ranch house, no one was on the porch. The place seemed quiet. After they parked and made their way to the house, they walked up the grand steps, across the large, stained-pine deck, and rang the doorbell. No one answered.

Scott was about to ring the bell again when the door opened. It was Gordon, and he was talking on the phone with someone. He smiled and waved for Scott and Sarah to come in. After they entered, Scott closed the door.

Sarah was almost giddy as she looked around at the magnificent western décor and enjoyed the view out the large picture windows.

Gordon kept talking as he motioned for them to follow him.

Scott and Sarah couldn't believe their eyes when they entered what must be Paddock's den. It was huge and lined from floor to ceiling with books on two walls and part of a third. The fourth wall consisted of windows and glassed double doors that looked over a beautifully landscaped backyard. They could see fancy rockwork surrounding a large swimming pool. Flowers were everywhere, along with many shade trees.

Scott sensed Gordon was talking about some big business deal. He and Sarah meandered around the den looking at the books. Some of the shelves also held small items that looked like they had come from all over the world. There were also quite a few plaques and awards.

Scott noticed the Paddocks had books on almost every subject, including science, success, history, art, philosophy, religion, and humor. They even had a section of books on sleight of hand tricks and card magic. Scott smiled. Then he glanced over and saw an open Bible on Gordon's desk. The text was surrounded by pen markings in multiple colors and extensive notes. Scott's mind raced back to his childhood. *Wow! That looks like Mr. Graham's Bible when he taught our Sunday school class,* he thought.

"I'm sorry for the delay," Gordon apologized after clicking his phone off. "I had to give my assistant some information about a business matter in Atlanta. You must be Sarah," Gordon said, offering a warm smile and his hand. "Scott has told me much about you."

Sarah shook Gordon's large hand and returned his smile. "It's so nice to meet you, Mr. Paddock. You have a wonderful ranch, and your home is gorgeous." Sarah noticed Paddock glancing over her shoulder toward the doorway.

His attention returned to Sarah. "Please call me Gordon. And, Sarah, I'd like you to meet my wife, Cody." He gestured to Sarah's right.

Sarah turned, not quite sure what to expect.

"Hello, Sarah!" Cody said as she approached and held out her hand. "I'm so glad you could come!"

Sarah was struck by her down-to-earth, warm smile. She looked like she'd just stepped out of a western magazine with her stylish jeans, cowgirl shirt, auburn hair, and country charm.

"Hello, Scott. It's good to see you again."

They shook hands.

Cody turned to Sarah. "How about you and I get acquainted? We'll let the menfolk talk while we go shopping—if you'd like."

Sarah nodded happily. She had on a big smile as she and Cody headed toward the door. Suddenly Sarah turned back and waved goodbye to Scott.

Cody glanced back and said coyly, "You know, Gordon, to be successful in shopping it takes more than seven seconds!"

The two women laughed and left together.

"Please sit down, Scott." Gordon motioned to a large, padded leather couch. He sat in one of the leather chairs and smiled. "How was your week?"

"You know, it was kind of fun. I found more Thinkers than I thought I would."

Gordon laughed. "What did you discover?"

"I guess the thing I noticed most was that the Thinkers seem to want a lot of facts and details when you talk to them."

"That's a good observation. Thinkers usually have a slow and deliberate thinking process. They are logical and like to take things step-by-step. They have a tendency to be very deductive. How do you think that would affect your encounters with them as clients?"

"Well, they would probably like to be given a sheet of paper with lots of details about the house I'm showing. Information like the size of each room, added features, price, schools and shopping centers in the neighborhood, things like that."

"Anything else?"

"I bet they wouldn't appreciate being pushed into a hurried decision. They would probably like time to think their decision over. They'd most likely be interested in seeing a number of different houses before making a decision...even if they really like the first house I show them."

"Very insightful. What type of professions do you envision Thinkers leaning toward?"

"Maybe professors or teachers of some kind?"

"Right. They could also be artists, doctors, or in the engineering field. They are attracted to professions that are specific and detail oriented. Thinkers are knowledgeable, very rational, sometimes reserved, and often cautious. They don't want to make a bad or wrong decision."

"That reminds me of what one Thinker said to his wife as they were walking around at an open house I held last weekend. He said, 'We need to look before we leap.'"

"That sounds like a Thinker, all right. They also say things like 'People don't plan to fail; they fail to plan.'"

Scott nodded.

"Thinkers are really specialists at heart. To them, progress must be measurable by activity. They are often motivated by the need to be right and to save face in situations that don't go as planned. They especially appreciate leaders and salespeople who give details. If you want to help them make a decision about any purchase, you need to give them facts. You must present evidence that convinces them that what they are considering is valid and makes good sense." Gordon rose from his chair and went to his large, carved, wooden desk. He opened a drawer and pulled out a sheet of paper. "Here, let me give you something that might help you understand the social style of Thinkers. It's a list of their positive traits and a list of their negative reactions."

Scott took the paper and read the lists.

"Scott, remember when we talked about the 'Seven Seconds to Success'?"

"Yes."

"Well, with Thinkers you *read* their body language in the first few seconds. Their heads have a tendency to be rigid. They may look away and not make or maintain a lot of eye contact. Their smiles might be somewhat reserved. They tend to have a tentative walk, and their postures may seem a little stiff or formal."

"Okay, I've seen that before in people, but I'm not sure what to do with the information."

"That comes in the next few seconds. You *observe* and *recognize* their characteristics. You do this by listening to what they say or noticing how they respond to what was said. Do they seem knowledgeable? Are they cautious and reserved? Do they come across as rational and detailed?"

Scott nodded in understanding.

"The next few seconds are when you have the opportunity to *relate* to the Thinker. Your goal is to become what I call 'precise' or 'informational.' This is the time you want to be very factual and to the point. You want to be calm in your presentation and not come on too strong. You should be deliberate in the order of what you say. You will notice Thinkers listening and evaluating what you are sharing. And it's important to be composed. By that I mean you don't want to be too emotional. Don't oversell using the pressure of feelings. It's facts and particulars that will win the day when it comes to Thinkers."

Scott absorbed what Gordon was saying.

"John Adams said, 'Facts are stubborn things; and whatever may be our wishes, our inclinations, or the dictates of our passions, they cannot alter the state of facts and evidence.' Thinkers live in that world."

Scott was in deep thought about how he had not been meeting the needs of the Thinkers that had come to his open houses. He realized he had pushed the feeling and emotional sides of the homes and neighborhoods, but he had not provided the detailed facts and advantages of the houses.

Gordon continued. "You see, Scott, the Thinker would really respond in a positive way to something Peter Drucker said. He was sharing on the importance of good evidence: 'Once the facts are clear, the decisions jump out at you.'"

"I can see how my not having the ability to *read, observe,* and *recognize* social styles has negatively affected my sales performance."

"On that note, I think you're ready for your next assignment. I want you to spend the next two weeks looking at the 'Tellers' in your life. They're the no-nonsense, bottom-line type of personalities. Do you know any of them?"

"My boss at Sears is one of those. I'll use him as my first case study."

Gordon laughed heartily. "You'll probably find that you'll do better at your job at Sears too when you get these social styles down." He paused before continuing. "Tellers are easy to spot, Scott. For example, President Theodore Roosevelt was a very opinionated and outspoken person. So was Harry S. Truman. The actor Clint Eastwood also falls into this category. A classic Teller in the comics would be Lucy from the *Peanuts* comic strip. She was always telling Charlie Brown and others what to do. The character Dr. McCoy in the *Star Trek* series was most certainly of the Teller type of personality. He said things like, 'What! Am I your nursemaid, Jim?'

"The apostle Paul from the Bible is an example of someone who had definite thoughts about God, life, and moral living. He was quite outspoken on many subjects. Once you start looking for Tellers, you will have no problem finding them. They are candid, frank, and sometimes very blunt."

"I think I know a number of those personalities. I may even know one of them too personally. Sarah sometimes accuses me of not being very tactful."

"Well, it will be interesting to see what you come up with."

Gordon handed Scott a sheet of paper entitled "Relating to the Thinker" before continuing. "Maybe these thoughts about Do's and Don'ts for Thinkers will help you at your next open house. Next time we get together, it will need to be in Anaheim. I have to be there on some business. I'll give you a call to set up the time. Does that sound like it will work for you?"

"Sure! I'll look forward to it," Scott affirmed.

As Gordon rose, he noticed a slight hesitation in Scott. He didn't say anything because he knew silence has a way of helping people put together their thoughts.

Finally, Scott spoke. "I see you have a Bible on your desk with lots of markings and notes."

Gordon smiled gently. "Yes. It's my guidebook for life."

Scott looked puzzled.

"You see, that book helps me in all of my relationships—with people at home and at work. It shows me how to deal with their emotions, such as anger and fear. It gives me direction on how to develop patience and speak kindly in all circumstances. Do you read the Bible, Scott?"

"Not really. Our family wasn't very religious. I went to Sunday school for a short time when I was a child. We seldom went to church as a family—except for weddings."

"That's quite common," Gordon said good-naturedly.

"Sarah reads the Bible, and she has encouraged me to go to church. But I've been busy on Sundays doing open houses."

Gordon went over to his bookshelves and pulled down a Bible. He handed it to Scott. "This is a *Life Application Bible*. It has many practical notes to help people understand how the Bible relates to everyday life. I'd like to give it to you."

"Why, thank you, Gordon."

"Just for fun, let me suggest a couple of things for you to read. I encourage you to start reading the book of John first. It will give you a good idea of who Jesus was and how he can affect your life and future."

"I've heard of that book. It's in the New Testament, isn't it?"

"Yes, the fourth book. The other book I suggest reading is Proverbs in the Old Testament. It is very practical and reveals how to get along with people of every type. I think you'll find it quite interesting and helpful."

"Thank you for this gift. I'll read those two sections."

"Great! In the meantime, let's go for a horseback ride around the ranch while we wait for the ladies to return."

Thinker Social Style

Positives	Behavior and Skills	Negatives
Aesthetic	Less assertive	Critical
Conscientious	Less responsive	Impractical
Exacting	More controlled	Indecisive
Gifted	Reserved	Legalistic
Idealistic	(an asker)	Moody
Industrious	Task oriented	Negative
Loyal	Technique	Persecution prone
Orderly	specialist	Picky
Perfectionist		Rigid
Persistent		Self-centered
Self-disciplined		Stuffy
Self-sacrificing		Theoretical
Sensitive		Touchy
Serious		Unsociable

Relating to the Thinker

Do's	Don'ts
Allow time for questions	Be disorganized
Be specific	Come on too strong
Give an organized pitch	Discredit their information
Provide lots of facts	Exaggerate
Stress quality	Fight with them
Talk slowly	Get personal
Talk softly	Overwhelm them
Use logical persuasion	Push them to buy
Validate their own research	Stare them down
	Talk loudly

Insight

· · · · · · · · · · · · ·

Facts are stubborn things;
and whatever may be our wishes,
our inclinations, or the dictates of
our passions, they cannot alter the state
of facts and evidence.

JOHN ADAMS

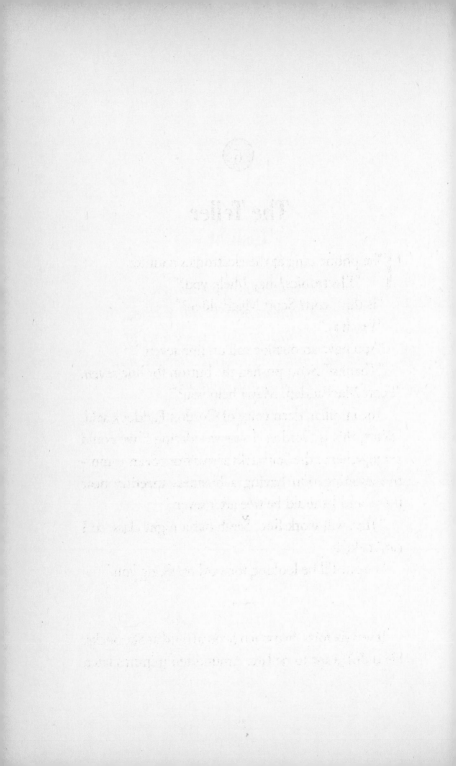

6

The Teller

The phone rang at the electronics counter.

"Electronics, may I help you?"

"Is this Scott? Scott MacFadden?"

"Yes, it is."

"You have an outside call on line seven."

"Thanks!" Scott pushed the button for line seven. "Scott MacFadden. May I help you?"

The familiar, deep voice of Gordon Paddock said, "Scott, this is Gordon. I was wondering if we could get together at the Starbucks across from Sears tomorrow evening. I'm having a business meeting near there, and I should be free after seven."

"That will work fine. Sarah has a night class, so I can make it."

"Great. I'll be looking forward to seeing you."

———※———

It was six forty-five when Scott arrived at Starbucks. He didn't want to be late. Around ten minutes later, he saw Gordon's sleek, black BMW drive into the parking lot.

I'll bet he's never late for anything, Scott decided.

Gordon had his usual broad smile on when he came through the door. His black suit, white shirt, and red tie certainly looked like a power outfit. It matched Paddock's overpowering presence. There was something about him that attracted people's attention. Paddock had a manila folder in his hand.

Scott made sure that he bought the coffee. He didn't want Gordon to think he was freeloading every chance he could.

Paddock gave a slight smile and had a twinkle in his eye when Scott insisted on buying. "Why, thank you, Scott. I can sure use a cup of coffee after my last meeting. You know, we Tellers need a little caffeine to keep us going."

They both laughed.

"Tell you what. I'll find a table and you get the coffee."

"That sounds good, Gordon."

"I like regular coffee, no cream or sugar," Gordon said before turning to locate a place to sit.

Scott went to get the coffee. When he returned, he handed Gordon his and sat down.

"Tell me, Scott, did you meet some outspoken Tellers during the last two weeks?"

"I observed a number of them. Their body language is a little more up front and evident. Their heads seem to be consistently up. It's like they are on full alert. Their eyes look ahead, and they move like they are working toward some goal. Many of them had a friendly yet businesslike kind of smile. Although I noticed that a few seemed preoccupied and didn't smile. Those people seemed more super-focused, and they didn't always pay attention to those who weren't in their goal pathway. They walked in a brisk manner. It struck me that they were in a hurry. With regard to their posture, they came across as confident and in charge or in control of the situation."

"Those are very good observations of body language, Scott. Did you discover any other characteristics the Tellers shared?"

"Yes. They all seemed to be pretty assertive. My guess is that it's an outgrowth of their confidence. I was impressed at how insightful and discerning they seemed to be. They processed information very rapidly and came to conclusions quickly. They had a unique objectivity when it came to evaluating ideas. It was like they could instinctively discern the right course of action. And speaking of action, the Tellers all seem to be high achievers. They also use their time in an organized manner."

"There is no question that Tellers are people of action. I'm reminded of a very action-oriented president named Theodore Roosevelt. He said, 'We are face-to-face with our destiny, and we must meet it with high and resolute courage. For us is the life of action, of strenuous performance of duty; let us live in the harness, striving mightily; let us rather run the risk of wearing out than rusting out.' Was there anything else you noted?"

"It seemed like the Tellers have a tendency to jump quickly to the bottom line in most discussions. They didn't come across as having much patience for those who don't get to the point quickly. It was almost like they steamrolled over people to gain control and get something accomplished."

"Have you met some Tellers while selling real estate?"

"Yes, and I felt like they were either pushy or very matter of fact. I responded negatively to their 'military' type of response, like I was a private talking to a general. I felt a little rebellious in their presence, and I think they picked up on my reaction. They didn't spend too much time with me. As I look back, I can see how my response probably cost me some sales. I'm beginning to see that their behavior and attitude weren't personal. They were just trying to get to their goal, and I wasn't helping them achieve it."

"Those are great insights. Tellers are certainly get-to-the-point specialists, for sure. They measure their progress by results, not talk. Their strongest motivation is to save time. They want to get things accomplished in a hurry. If you want Tellers to get something done, give them options or alternatives they can choose between. They will then determine the shortest point between the idea and the goal."

"It seems like one of the Tellers' biggest problems is that they have a tendency not to listen. They are more focused on their plan rather than other people's ideas," responded Scott.

"Sounds like you're gaining some good clues to relating to people. Tellers have a tendency to go into fields of work that are advisory in nature. They often excel as consultants. Many lawyers seem to have this personality. Tellers can be found in areas that require the management of people. They are often administrators in organizations."

Gordon started to open the folder he'd brought with him, but then he stopped.

"I have a couple of sheets of information I brought for you. The first will give you an overview of the positive and negative traits of the Teller's social style. The second are some Do's and Don'ts relating to Tellers. Before I show them to you, let me clarify several definitions so I can be sure we're on the same page. There is a term called 'social style.' Your social style is simply your natural inclinations. These are what you're born with. It's sometimes referred to as temperament. Your personality, on the other hand, is how you individually express your inherited social style. Personality can be affected by your environment, whereas your social style remains fairly constant. Being a Thinker, Teller, Toucher, or Talker is inherited and is pretty consistent. Personality varies. It's like your fingerprints. Everyone has them, but they are individually unique."

"Do you mean 'once a Teller always a Teller'?" Scott asked.

"Yes. The same is true for being a Thinker, a Toucher, and a Talker. The difference between various individual Tellers is how they *express* their Telling temperament. That individual expression is commonly referred to as their *personality*. Each personality is different."

Scott nodded.

Paddock went on. "The other term I want to mention is 'character.' Your character is the quality of your individual personality. It's affected by your morals, your values, and your ethics. It's possible for a Teller to be a person of high morals and high values. It's also possible for a Teller to be a person of low morals and low values. Adolph Hitler was a good example of a Teller with low morals and values."

Paddock opened the manila folder, took out the sheet of paper, and handed it to Scott. He was silent as Scott studied it for a moment. Then Gordon continued. "One of the things that's easy for Tellers is making decisions. They don't have much patience for those who can't decide. Thinkers might say, 'I don't want to make a decision until I have all the facts.' Tellers know that if they wait until they have all the facts, it's no longer a decision—it's a *conclusion*. Decisions are made based on the facts available at a specific point in time. That's why they are called decisions. Texas businessman T. Boone Pickens said, 'Be willing to make decisions. That's the most important quality of a good leader. Don't fall victim to what I call the "ready-aim-aim-aim-aim" syndrome. You must be willing to fire.'" Paddock paused.

The silence was uncomfortable for Scott. *Gordon doesn't seem to mind silence. It's like he believes silence can bring insights or something,* Scott decided.

"Are you ready for your next assignment?"

"You bet," replied Scott. "This is interesting and exciting, as well as helpful."

"During the next two weeks, I want you to find and observe 'Touchers.' They are very easygoing people who seem to get along with everyone. Think singers, movie stars, and television personalities. Bing Crosby is a prime example of a relaxed Toucher. Mahatma Gandhi, the leader of India during its battle for independence, believed in nonviolent action. He brought about many reforms using diplomacy and nonviolent methods. President Gerald Ford was also in the Toucher category.

"In the original *Star Trek* series, Scotty, in the engine room, is the picture of an individual who enjoys helping and pleasing those he works with. Bible personality Barnabas was very diplomatic and endeavored to soothe ruffled relationships. That's what Touchers are good at. Another example is the cartoon character Winnie-the-Pooh. He tried to make peace with all his friends and neighbors."

"I've met some Winnie-the-Pooh people," Scott said, laughing.

"I'll give you a call week after next to set up a meeting," Gordon said. "We can go over the results of your assignment then."

Scott shook Gordon's hand and paused. "Gordon, I really appreciate the time and interest you are pouring into me. It means a lot to me and my wife. And by the way, I read the book of John like you suggested."

"What did you think?"

"I was really impressed by Jesus and what he had to say."

"Did anything in particular catch your attention?"

"Yes. He gave the impression that he was God's son, and that people who came to him would never hunger or thirst again."

"Do you think he was talking about some kind of food and water?"

"No. I could tell he was talking about someone who was hungry and thirsty for God."

"Why did that impress you?"

"I guess because I think there is something missing in my life. I think there may be some type of void I need to fill."

"Scott, do you remember flying a kite as a child? You ran with the kite held high until the wind caught it, and then it soared into the sky? If you had a long string, the kite would rise higher and higher. Eventually it would be so high that it seemed to disappear. The only way you could tell the kite was still there was by the tug on the string caused by the wind. In the same way, God gives a tug on the strings of your heart. Something inside you senses God is calling you. Do you feel that tug?"

"I think so. I'm more interested in spiritual things right now."

"That's a good thing. Jesus said, 'For what will it profit a man if he gains the whole world and forfeits his soul? Or what will a man give in exchange for his soul?' By that, Jesus is simply saying that there is more to life than material goods and success. He's saying it's dangerous to not consider the deeper purposes of life. Have you ever wondered what life is all about or if God has a plan for you?"

Scott nodded his head before admitting, "Yes, I've had those thoughts."

"The Bible says God cares about you, and he has a purpose for your life. He wants to come to your aid and help fill the void inside you. According to the book of Matthew, Jesus said, 'Come to Me, all you who labor and are heavy laden, and I will give you rest. Take My yoke upon you and learn from Me, for I am gentle and lowly in heart, and you will find rest for your souls. For My yoke is easy and My burden is light.'"

"How does someone 'come to Jesus'? How do I find this rest?"

"In the book of Romans we are told,

> 'If you confess with your mouth Jesus as Lord, and believe in your heart that God raised Him from the dead, you will be saved; for with the heart a person believes, resulting in righteousness, and with the mouth he confesses, resulting in salvation. For the Scripture says, "Whoever believes in Him will not be disappointed." '

"The apostle Paul made it pretty clear, didn't he?" Gordon said.

"It sounds rather simple. Is it really that easy?"

"Yes, it is. And you can pray that prayer anytime. You can be in a group of people, in a church, or all by yourself in your house. I suggest you read the book of John again and keep reading in the book of Proverbs. When you think you're ready to make a decision for Christ, you can pray and God will answer."

"Okay…but being raised from the dead…and making Jesus my Lord—those are some heavy ideas."

"Becoming a Christian isn't that hard. It's simply turning away from sin and turning to Christ. It's called 'repentance.' John Locke, considered the intellectual founder of our country, stated it this way:

> 'Repentance is a hearty sorrow for our past misdeeds, and is a sincere resolution and endeavor, to the utmost of our power, to conform all of our actions to the law of God. It does not consist in one single act of sorrow, but in doing works meet for repentance; in a sincere obedience to the law of Christ for the remainder of our lives.'

"Does that make sense to you, Scott?" Paddock could see Scott was processing everything that had been said. "Scott, why don't you continue reading and thinking about what we've discussed. If you have any questions, I'll be happy to discuss them when we get together next time."

Teller Social Style

Positives	Behavior and Skills	Negatives
Active	Control specialist	Crafty
Courageous	More assertive	Domineering
Decisive	Less responsive	Inconsiderate
Determined	More controlled	Insensitive
Efficient	Outspoken (teller)	Opinionated
Independent	Task-oriented	Prejudiced
Leader		Proud
Optimistic		Pushy
Practical		Sarcastic
Productive		Severe
Self-confident		Tough
Strong-willed		Unforgiving
Visionary		Unsympathetic

Relating to the Teller

Do's	Don'ts
Ask their opinion	Argue with them
Be brief	Be passive
Get to the point	Belabor your points
Let them stay in control	Chitchat
Make your presentation quickly	Go off on tangents
Show confidence	Pressure them
Stay businesslike	Talk about your personal life
Think fast	Try to overpower them

Insights

· · · · · · · · · · · · · ·

We are face-to-face with our destiny, and we must meet it with high and resolute courage. For us is the life of action, of strenuous performance of duty; let us live in the harness, striving mightily; let us rather run the risk of wearing out than rusting out.

THEODORE ROOSEVELT

Be willing to make decisions. That's the most important quality of a good leader. Don't fall victim to what I call the "ready-aim-aim-aim syndrome." You must be willing to fire.

T. BOONE PICKENS

7

The Toucher

Scott had just put the last few boxes of electronic games on the shelf when he heard a voice behind him.

"Will you please help me?"

He turned around, fully expecting someone to want one of the games he'd just put on the shelf. To his surprise he faced the large frame of Gordon Paddock.

"Gordon! I didn't expect to find you shopping at Sears."

"Actually, I was in the neighborhood and thought I would drop by to see if we could set up another time to talk."

"Sure! What would work in your schedule?"

"I'm doing another 'Seven Seconds to Success' seminar nearby next Tuesday afternoon. Why don't you join me at Starbucks afterward?"

"Tuesday would be great! What time would you like to meet?"

"Let's shoot for six thirty. Will that work for you?"

"Sure, that will be great," Scott answered.

They shook hands, and Paddock disappeared into the crowd of shoppers. Scott was deeply impressed that Gordon had sought him out at Sears. He was excited and couldn't wait to tell Sarah that his mentor had come to see him to set up their next meeting.

———

It was six twenty-five when Paddock's BMW drove into the Starbucks' parking lot. As he entered the door, he was smiling but he looked a little tired. Scott greeted him, they ordered coffee, and then sat down at a table.

"Well, did you discover some Touchers?" Gordon asked immediately.

"Quite a few of them, actually. I noticed that a number of them didn't hold their heads as rigid as the Thinkers or weren't as goal directed as the Tellers. Often their heads seemed to drop down a little. Their eye movements and eye contact gave me the impression they might be a little unsure of themselves."

"What about their smiles and the way they walked?"

"That was interesting. They had gentle and kind smiles. Their walk was not brisk, like the Tellers. It was more casual. Their posture indicated a sort of uncertainty. It's hard to put into words."

"I think you're doing fine. What particular characteristics did you notice?"

"As a rule of thumb, I saw the Touchers as very supportive people. They seemed to like to please people and be part of a team. They came across as willing, agreeable, and very compassionate."

"Those are good observations, Scott. You often find Touchers in the teaching professions. They make good counselors because they're diplomatic. They encourage peace at home or where they work. Many Touchers lean toward the healthcare or service-oriented industries. Often you will find them as secretaries or assistants to leaders."

"They come across as if they genuinely like to do kind acts for people."

"That is very true. They do get a great deal of satisfaction from helping others. Touchers are good at being 'support specialists.' They do best when given attention or recognition for their service. Their motivation is to save and heal relationships. Albert Schweitzer said, 'Constant kindness can accomplish much. As the sun makes ice melt, kindness causes misunderstanding, mistrust and hostility to evaporate.'"

"If I had a Toucher come to an open house, what would be my best response?" Scott asked.

"Since relationships are important to them, it's good to be personable and attentive to their needs. A friendly and cooperative spirit is essential. Charles Schwab said, 'Lead the life that will make you kindly and friendly to everyone about you, and you will be surprised what a happy life you will live.' You don't want to put pressure on Touchers for decisions. They might say yes just to please you, but inside they feel your pressure. They'll disappear and not return as soon as they can get away from you."

"I think I've put too much pressure on the Touchers who have come to my open houses. Now I know why they didn't come back," Scott admitted.

There was a long pause as Gordon allowed Scott to ponder his last statement.

"There is a fourth personality type I'd like you to observe next. You've looked at the Thinkers, the Tellers, and the Touchers. Now, I want you to consider 'the Talkers.' When you think of Talkers, entertainers like Bob Hope or Jay Leno come to mind. On the *Star Trek* series, Captain Kirk was a very outspoken and volatile personality, willing to share his emotions and charismatic presence with everyone. In the cartoons,

Donald Duck illustrates the Talker. When it comes to people in the Bible, the apostle Peter is a classic example of a Talker."

"This is fun! I'm ready to go out and identify the Talkers," Scott asserted.

"I'm glad you're enjoying the process. It is all part of the 'Seven Seconds to Success.' You're learning how to identify people's social styles quickly. I'm sure it will translate into successful sales for you in the days ahead."

"It's already helped me," Scott said with a smile.

"I hope you don't mind that this meeting is so short. It's been a long day. Why don't we get together in two weeks at the ranch. That will give you some time to gather information about Talkers."

"No problem," Scott said. "And two weeks sounds just fine. Our usual one o'clock?"

"Perfect!" Gordon said.

After finishing their coffee, both men headed to their cars.

On his drive home, Scott thought about how fortunate he was to have Gordon Paddock as a mentor.

Toucher Social Style

Positives	Behavior and Skills	Negatives
Agreeable	Less assertive	Awkward
Calm	More emoting	Blasé
Conservative	More responsive	Conforming
Dependable	Relationship oriented	Dependent
Diplomatic	Reserved (asker)	Fearful
Dry humor	Support specialist	Indecisive
Easygoing		Indolent
Efficient		Ingratiating
Likeable		Selfish
Organized		Self-protective
Practical		Spectator
Reluctant leader		Stingy
Respectful		Stubborn
Supportive		Unbothered
Willing		Unsure

Relating to the Toucher

Do's	Don'ts
Be friendly	Be insensitive
Display patience	Be sarcastic
Empathize with their concerns	Become stressed
	Overwhelm them
Listen to them	Pressure them for a buying decision
Make them feel valued	
Show kindness	Put down their opinions
Smile	Rush them
Stay relaxed	Show impatience
Treat them gently	Talk loudly

Insights

· · · · · · · · · · · · · ·

Constant kindness can accomplish much.
As the sun makes ice melt, kindness
causes misunderstanding, mistrust
and hostility to evaporate.

ALBERT SCHWEITZER

———

Lead the life that will make you kindly and
friendly to everyone about you, and you will
be surprised what a happy life you will live.

CHARLES SCHWAB

8

The Talker

The two-hour drive to the ranch gave Scott time to think about how his life had been changing. He had become more and more aware of the actions of other people since meeting Gordon. Scott could tell that his ability to read body language had increased dramatically. And this knowledge was beginning to affect how he related to the needs of everyone he came into contact with. He also realized he was becoming less focused on his own desires. Sarah had even commented that she appreciated his more positive attitude. Their relationship had been good, but they seemed to be developing an even closer bond.

Scott could also sense that he was becoming more effective in real estate. One of his homes had closed, and two more were in escrow. Customers were responding to his concern for them and his helpfulness. They were trusting him.

As he drove down the white-fenced driveway, something caught Scott's eye. A person was riding a horse in one of the pastures. As Scott got closer, he could see that the man riding wasn't Gordon. This guy was much younger, and the way he sat in the saddle and the response of the horse made Scott think of John Wayne riding off into the sunset in an old Western.

Scott waved as he drove by, and the young man waved back. He then urged his horse on and galloped toward the stables.

———

"Good to see you, Scott!" Gordon greeted as they shook hands. Scott asked about the man on the horse. Gordon smiled and replied, "That's our youngest son, Jody. He manages the ranch since I am away quite a bit. He's just like his mom—he loves horses, and they love him."

"How many horses do you have on the ranch?" asked Scott.

"At this time there are twenty-three. Four of them belong to a neighbor. He's on vacation, so we're taking care of them. Let's sit on the porch to talk."

Scott sat down and looked over the lake and the green pastures. He hoped that someday he would have his own piece of property like this.

"Well, bring me up to speed. What have you discovered since we last met?"

Scott laughed and shook his head. "I had a real Talker come to my open house this last week. I could hear him coming before he rang the doorbell! I looked outside, and he was chatting with his wife as they were walking up the sidewalk path. His head was relaxed, and his eyes were looking toward the house. His smile was highly responsive, and he was talking a mile a minute. He had an energetic walk, and his posture gave the impression of being approachable and unrestrained."

"It does sound like a Talker."

"When I opened the door, he greeted me before I could say anything. He said, 'Hi, I'm Ken, and this is my wife, Melba. This house looks great from the outside. We'd like to come in and take a look.' It was almost like he was trying to sell me on the idea."

Paddock laughed. "You know, Scott, Talkers are extroverts. They are the continual optimists who see a rose with every thorn. If a Talker's house was on fire, he would say, 'Since the house is on fire, let's warm ourselves.' They're very charismatic, friendly, and enthusiastic."

"He and his wife came in and immediately started asking me where I was from and how long I'd been in the real estate business. They must have stayed an hour. And that's unusual for an open house."

"One thing is certain about Talkers—they do have positive attitudes. I think George Bernard Shaw must have been thinking about a Talker when he said, 'The people who get on in this world are the people who get up and look for the circumstances they want and, if they can't find them, make them.'"

Scott smiled and nodded.

Paddock continued. "Talkers do well in sales and marketing positions. You'll also find them owning businesses. They have an entrepreneurial spirit and are willing to take risks. Often you find Talkers in public service positions."

Scott grew serious for a moment. "In the past, I didn't get along very well with Talkers. I saw them as blowhards or motormouths. I could hardly get a word in edgewise. My reaction was to ignore them and hope they'd shut up or leave."

"And now?" asked Paddock.

"I'm beginning to appreciate them. They're just very friendly people. They are open and honest, and what you see is what you get with them."

"Being sociable is one of the Talkers' great qualities. Dale Carnegie said, 'You can make more friends in two months by becoming interested in other people than you can in two years by trying to get other people interested in you.' Solomon wrote, 'A man's discretion makes him slow to anger, and it is his glory to overlook a transgression.' That's in the book of Proverbs."

Scott nodded again. He appreciated Paddock taking an interest in him. "How should I respond to Talkers as potential clients?"

"Be positive and sociable with them. If they are energetic, you become a little more energetic. Talkers are very animated and make many gestures. They're great storytellers, and they are very compelling and emotional about any topic they're discussing. Focus on their needs and concerns. Be cheerful and interested."

"Are there any keys to dealing with all four social styles?"

"There are several. First, you have to be able to identify them by their body language. Posture is often a good clue. As a rule of thumb, Thinkers have a tendency to be stiff and formal. Tellers have a confident demeanor. Touchers can come across as uncertain. Talkers seem to be more open and approachable. This observation only takes a second. It's your first impression of someone. Trust that first impression."

"I'm a lot more aware of that now," Scott said. "Thanks to you."

"Next, listen to what they say. Thinkers talk about facts and details. Tellers go for the bottom line. Touchers are concerned about relationships. Talkers deal in feelings and emotions."

"That's a little more difficult for me to judge," Scott admitted.

"At first, it may seem confusing. But after a little while you'll become very adept at listening for personality clues. You'll be able to identify the social styles in seconds. It will become like second nature to you."

"How about my response once I think I know what their social styles are?"

"Now I'm going to introduce you to what I call the key words: precise, practical, personal, and positive. They're easily remembered as the '4 P's':

- With Thinkers, *be precise*. By that, I mean give them information, facts, and details.

- With Tellers, *be practical*. They don't want a lot of details. They appreciate the bottom line.

- With Touchers, *be personal*. Remember that relationships are very important to them.

- With Talkers, *be positive.* They are upbeat people who like other upbeat people."

"I like the '4 P's.' That's a very helpful way to remember how best to respond to the social styles. Are there any other things that would be good for me to know?"

"Yes, I think it would be important to know how to deal with someone who is having a bad day. I'm referring to when people are annoying and difficult to get along with. We all have days like that."

"That would be great. I have a few people in my life who always seem to be having bad days."

"We all do, Scott. For this assignment I want you to observe how the four social styles respond under the pressures of bad days."

"Great, Gordon. I'll do it!"

"Before you leave, here is a sheet of do's and don'ts when dealing with Talkers. Now, how about getting together in a couple of weeks at our usual Starbucks to review your findings? I have another seminar in Orange County, so we can meet during the evening if that will work out for you."

"I can meet you any evening. You're the one with the busy schedule," Scott asserted.

Talker Social Style

Positives	Behavior and Skills	Negatives
Ambitious	More assertive	Disorganized
Carefree	More emoting	Egotistical
Charismatic	More responsive	Exaggerates
Compassionate	Outspoken (a teller)	Excitable
Dramatic	Relationship oriented	Loud
Enthusiastic	Social specialist	Manipulative
Friendly		Obnoxious
Generous		Reactive
Outgoing		Restless
Responsive		Undependable
Stimulating		Undisciplined
Talkative		Unproductive
Warm		Weak-willed

Relating to the Talker

Do's	Don'ts
Add excitement	Be blasé
Ask about their interests	Be impersonal
Ask about their personal lives	Be stuffy
Be informal	Be very serious
Joke around with them	Bore them with details
Make a colorful presentation	Cut them short
Make it fun	Ignore them
Socialize with them	Neglect them
	Stay businesslike
	Talk slowly

Insight

· · · · · · · · · · · ·

*The people who get on in this world are
the people who get up and look for the
circumstances they want and,
if they can't find them, make them.*

GEORGE BERNARD SHAW

—⁓—

*You can make more friends in two months
by becoming interested in other people than
you can in two years by trying to get
other people interested in you.*

DALE CARNEGIE

—⁓—

*A man who has friends must
himself be friendly.*

SOLOMON, PROVERBS 18:24

9

The Bad Day

When Scott arrived at Starbucks, he could see Gordon Paddock sitting at one of the black, wrought-iron tables on the patio area outside.

Paddock smiled as Scott walked up. "Good evening, Scott. It's such a mild evening I thought we could grab an outside table."

"That's a great idea. It's too nice an evening to be inside. Do you want your usual black coffee?"

"Sure, Scott."

"I'll go get our drinks. I'll be right back." When he returned, Scott sat down and was the first to speak.

"That was quite an assignment you gave me. This is the first time I've ever looked for 'bad day' behavior."

Paddock laughed deeply. "I'm sure that's true. Usually people's bad-day behavior bumps into us rather than our searching for it. What did you discover?"

"Actually, I didn't have to look very far for it. Two days after our talk, my boss at Sears had one of his typical bad days. Not only does he oversee the electronics area, but he's been given a temporary assignment to cover the Housekeeping Department too."

"Sounds like he might be under a little stress," Paddock observed.

"That's for sure. He's the type who doesn't have much patience—especially with pushy customers. We had a sale on sheets, and the customers were almost out of control. They were grabbing for sheets as fast as they could, and my manager couldn't get them out of the cart quickly enough. One woman scratched his arm accidentally. I happened to walk by when the commotion was going on."

"What happened?"

"Well, when the woman scratched his arm, the manager jerked back and snarled, 'Back off!' All of the women froze for a moment and stared at him. He suddenly realized that was not the best way to win customers, so he tried to soften his angry approach. He said, 'Excuse me, ladies. Will you please allow me to take the sheets out of the cart before you select them?' It was a pretty intense situation. And it didn't really slow the shoppers down very much. They kept reaching for sheets and ignoring him. Finally he just stepped back and let them grab what they wanted until the cart was empty."

Paddock laughed again.

"When the manager came back to the stockroom, the air turned blue with his ranting and raving. He went on about women for at least five minutes. Everyone else in the room became very quiet. It's best not to cross him when he's upset."

"Each of the social styles responds differently to bad days," Gordon said. "The Thinkers have a tendency to withdraw from any kind of conflict. This is so they can give themselves time to go through the problem and come up with some kind of solution or response. They need as much information as possible to deal effectively with their distress. Often they won't respond at all. They let small conflicts build up. It's like they're putting their hurt and anger into a gunnysack—but they hold on to them. Occasionally, they'll dump the entire sack on an unsuspecting individual."

Scott chuckled. "I've been one of those unsuspecting individuals. My mother had a tendency to hold back her thoughts, and then all of a sudden she would dump a whole truckload. It was often a shock. We weren't aware that she was stuffing down so many things."

"It's best not to keep pushing Thinkers for a response or to insist on their increased participation before they have time to think. They're more systematic, so they approach problem solving with a step-by-step process. Slow down and be patient. They need time and space. It's best to give it to them."

"That would have made a big difference with my mother," Scott decided.

Paddock nodded. "The Tellers are different when they face conflict. If Tellers think they are beginning to lose control of a situation, they'll dig in their heels and try to dominate. They'll become loud, dogmatic, and overbearing. It's best to not compete with Tellers. Don't argue or debate with them—but don't back down either, even when they come on strong. Tellers respect people who hold their ground, even if those people don't agree with the Teller's position."

"I have a tendency to do that—to argue, I mean," Scott confessed.

"So do I," admitted Paddock. "Touchers react to conflict or having bad days in ways similar to Thinkers. They withdraw or become very quiet. Only their withdrawal isn't to contemplate the situation. Instead, it's to try to save the relationship at all costs—even if it means personal hurt. But don't be fooled. Their compliance is not a sign of commitment. Don't express anger to them, argue with them, or insist on your way. These responses will push them deeper into their pattern of acquiescence as they continue to struggle to save the relationship. Instead, the best thing to do is encourage them to share their feelings. Ask them for *constructive criticism* regarding the conflict. Tell them you want to work on the situation, but you need some concrete suggestions from them to help you. Work side by side with them through the problem-solving process. They will respond cautiously, so move slowly and be patient."

"That sounds like my father," said Scott. "He didn't like any type of conflict. He wanted everyone to be at peace. He was a very diplomatic individual."

"The last social style to consider is the Talker. Talkers face bad days by letting everyone know exactly how they feel when they feel it. They'll explode and sometimes even attack others verbally with their discontent. They'll not hesitate to chew you out and tell you what they don't like—and they'll do so with gusto. It doesn't help to try to evaluate their outbursts or defend yourself intellectually. Talkers' behavior is emotion based. Don't let them draw you into their tantrums. It doesn't help to shout back because they usually have stronger lungs and will shout you down. Instead, listen sympathetically and accept their emotions without getting emotionally involved. Let them get their emotions out of their system. If you block their venting, you may provoke an even greater explosion. Once they get their emotions off their chests, help them focus on creative ways to handle the problem."

"Okay. Now I've been exposed to all of those different bad-day reactions. How should I respond to them when I'm working with them?"

"The first thing I suggest is for you to be alert to how *you* are feeling. Do you feel your tension level rising? If you do, take control of your feelings and thoughts. Don't let the other person's behavior trigger your bad-day behavior. Charles Swindoll said, 'Only 10 percent of life is what happens to you. The other 90 percent is how you choose to react to it. You can choose your responses.'"

"That sounds easier to do than it is!"

"No question about that, Scott. King Solomon wrote, 'He who restrains his words has knowledge, and he who has a cool spirit is a man of understanding.' It's important to be alert to the subtle behaviors of Thinkers and Touchers. They'll withdraw and hold things back. On the other hand, Tellers and Talkers will let everything out."

"Those are good key points to remember."

"Yes, and may I add that a person's bad-day behavior may not be directed at you personally? Sometimes whatever you said or did that provoked the negative behavior was simply the last straw. They could have other pressures that may have been mounting up, and you just happened to be the one to feel the brunt of their bad day. Instead of responding defensively by saying something like 'You're sure a grouch today,' you might say, 'It sounds like you're having a difficult day. May I be of help?'"

"I don't know if I can think that fast and have that positive of a response when I'm being attacked."

"No one said it would be easy, Scott," Gordon admitted. "Conflict can be an opportunity for growth or a tool for the destruction of relationships. There is another proverb that says, 'A man's discretion makes him slow to anger, and it is his glory to overlook a transgression.' Sometimes we have to have broad shoulders and let negative things roll off them."

"It's going to take me a little time to develop those broad shoulders!"

"It's not a once-and-for-all action, Scott. We all have to work at it day by day. Let me share with you two other areas of conflict between people. They are 'pace' and 'priority.'"

"What do you mean by 'pace' and 'priority'?"

"People think and move at different speeds. Some people operate at a slower pace, carefully plotting and planning before acting. Other people think and move at a faster pace, acting and responding impulsively. Slower-paced people often feel uncomfortable with those who act first and think second. Faster-paced people are often annoyed by those who are indecisive and slow to act. A faster-paced person and a slower-paced person will look at the same circumstances through entirely different eyes. And by the way—they often marry each other!"

Scott chuckled. "Now I understand exactly what you're saying. It sounds like Sarah and me."

Paddock grinned. "Thinkers and Touchers are usually slower paced and think in a deductive, methodical, step-by-step process. On the other hand, Tellers and Talkers are faster paced, inductive, more intuitive, and more immediate in their thinking. Both groups have little patience for the other."

"I'm beginning to realize why I have a hard time getting along with some people."

"That's understandable." Paddock paused to drink some coffee. "The second reason why people become irritated with each other's behavior is 'priorities.' Some people regard tasks as more important than relationships. Others prioritize relationships over tasks. Who is right and who is wrong? Or is one thing more important than the other? It all depends on the person you're talking to. The issue of priorities is the biggest point of contention between people who are Thinkers and Tellers and people who are Touchers and Talkers. There is a constant rub between those who want to achieve and accomplish and those who want to relate and get along."

"Wow, you really hit the nail on the head! I see myself as a task-oriented person. No wonder I've had a hard time with people who are more relationship oriented."

"That's a great insight, Scott. A major part of learning to get along with someone is to understand your own perspective, and then to understand the other person's perspective. It takes effort and energy. When I begin to see situations through the eyes of another person, my compassion develops. I become slower at judging the person's behavior."

"I can see that," said Scott. "But what about my intentions?"

"What do you mean?"

"Isn't it possible to take all this information and simply use it as a manipulation technique to get people to buy what I'm selling?"

"Well, Scott, I suppose the short answer is yes. It is possible to manipulate people rather than care about their needs. However, that type of behavior will catch up with a person eventually. At some point people will realize they've been used, cheated, and lied to. When that happens, your reputation is destroyed, people's trust in you ends, and your earnings cease. Remember, there is the Golden Rule we talked about: 'Do to others what you would have them do to you.'"

Scott nodded.

"You see, everything comes down to character, honesty, and integrity. Is your motivation to truly be interested in others and help meet their needs? Or is it to satisfy your own desires? A life of selfishness is empty, unfulfilling, and destructive. Charles Kingsley said,

> 'If you wish to be miserable, think about yourself; about what you want, what you like, what respect people ought to pay you, what people think of you; and then to you nothing will be pure. You will spoil everything you touch; you will make sin and misery for yourself out of everything God sends you; you will be wretched as you choose.'"

Paddock reached into his briefcase that was on the ground by his chair. He pulled out a notebook and handed it to Scott. "Here's a notebook I put together for you about 'Seven Seconds to Success.' It's a summary of what we've discussed. I'm sure you'll find the information helpful and very good for reviewing the principles."

Scott was silent for a moment.

Paddock looked at him, a warm smile on his lips.

"You know, Gordon, your insights and your wisdom have really helped me gain a new perspective about people and about me. It has transformed how I deal with customers at Sears and in my real estate job. What I don't understand is why you've been so kind to spend so much time with me. Will you tell me?"

Paddocks green eyes sparkled. "Do you remember when I said you remind me of someone I once knew?"

"Yes…"

"That person was me when I was just starting out in business. I'm glad I could help you. I've enjoyed spending time with you."

"Could we possibly get together one more time?" Scott asked. "I have a few more questions and ideas I'd like to discuss with you."

Gordon smiled. "Sure, Scott. Review the notebook, and then give me a call. We'll arrange a meeting then."

Insights

· · · · · · · · · · · · · ·

*Only 10 percent of life is what happens to
you. The other 90 percent is how you choose
to react to it. You can choose your responses.*

Charles Swindoll

---

*He who restrains his words has knowledge,
and he who has a cool spirit
is a man of understanding.*

Solomon, Proverbs 17:27

---

*A man's discretion makes him slow to anger,
and it is his glory to overlook
a transgression.*

Solomon, Proverbs 19:11

The Notebook

Gordon Paddock
Paddock Enterprises

7 Seconds to Success is a program that reaches out to meet the needs of people. It is formulated around the Golden Rule as taught by Jesus: "So in everything, do to others what you would have them do to you" (Matthew 7:12). This is not always easy to demonstrate, especially in the face of criticism or rejection. But we can choose to respond lovingly to others even when we don't feel like it. Some might say that if we did that when we didn't feel like it, we'd be hypocrites. We suggest that we would not be hypocrites. Instead, we'd be responsible people demonstrating responsible behavior.

If we all waited to perform loving activities until we felt like doing them, there would be a lot of neglected activities. For example, when our children are young, we probably don't feel like changing dirty diapers or getting up in the middle of the night to care for a sick child. Those are loving deeds performed apart from loving feelings. And we don't always feel like going to work, especially when we're sick. Are we hypocrites because we go to work when we don't feel like it? No, we are responsible people doing what needs to be done.

When it comes to getting along with people, there are times when we must respond to people in a loving way, not because we feel like doing so, but because it is the loving thing do. Individuals with hearts of concern are willing to adapt their behavior to meet the needs and questions of others, no matter how they feel about doing so. This concern for others seeks to reduce the stress and tension caused by bad-day behaviors.

This deep concern for people also seeks unity between the various social styles. Understanding that people may have different thinking processes and viewpoints than we do gives us the ability to adapt to the differences in others. It allows us to look for ways to experience productive interchanges and cooperation.

We don't need to negate our own personalities or deny our own social style to perform acts of love and concern. Nor does performing positive activities for others mean that we give up our own goals. On the contrary, we try to reach our goals by adapting our social styles to make others feel more comfortable.

Yes, we can modify our behavior and reduce tension from selfish motives. For example, we may laugh at the boss's jokes even though they aren't funny so he will like us and help advance our careers. This is not concern—it's manipulation on our part. We all know how to change our behavior to manipulate, exploit, use, or control others.

Instead, our motivation for responsible behavioral change needs to be love and concern for others. Loving interaction from a positive motive will be marked by sensitivity, respect, integrity, honesty, understanding, harmony, and communication. In adapting to meet the desires of others, each social style has its own particular needs.

Responding to Thinkers

- Thinkers don't appreciate people who come on too strong. Speak softly and slowly to Thinkers.

- Thinkers are more task oriented, and they appreciate discussions about achievement. Talk to them about reachable goals.

- Thinkers are deductive in their thinking process. Be sure to meet their needs for facts, data, time lines, and step-by-step procedures.

- Don't expect quick decisions from Thinkers. Give them time to reflect on information before they have to decide.

- Thinkers want to know how things work. They appreciate detailed instructions.

- Thinkers have a strong need to be right and to make right decisions. They would rather make no decision than a wrong one. Help them realize that it is impossible to make perfect decisions all the time. Help them relax and encourage them during the decision-making process.

- Thinkers sometimes feel awkward in relationships. Help them save face by not putting too much pressure on them in social situations.

- Exercise patience when dealing with Thinkers. When they talk, they often give out more information than necessary. They will explain their positions with great detail. Their presentations of material may be so loaded with facts that they are boring and difficult to follow. They have a strong need to explain themselves clearly and completely. You may need to listen to more material than you would like to assure Thinkers you are listening and you care.

- Don't oversell your ideas or overstate your position to Thinkers. They have a strong sense of logic, and they can quickly identify reasonable facts. Be clear and specific.

- Encourage and praise Thinkers for their wise planning, efficient techniques, and conservative nature.

Responding to Tellers

- Tellers appreciate people who make their points clearly and concisely. Try not to bore them with a lot of details. Get to the bottom line quickly.

- Tellers are intuitive thinkers and will trust their hunches. Don't give them a big sales pitch. If your ideas or suggestions seem valid, Tellers will immediately accept them. However, they may not admit the validity of your ideas because they need to remain in control.

- Since Tellers like to be leaders, let them choose their methods or paths of response. Tell them the goal you would like to achieve, and give them options or alternatives for reaching that goal. Let them use the information to chart their own course.

- Tellers want to know what is going on, what needs to be accomplished, and what your ideas are. They are interested in the answers to how, who, why, and when questions. Be sure to let them know what your goals are. They will tell you if they can or will reach them.

- Tellers struggle with impatience. Since they process information and accomplish tasks quickly, they don't have much patience with those who think or work slowly. Try to increase your pace around Tellers. They appreciate saving time because they want to get on to their many other tasks.

- Since Tellers move at such a quick pace, try to keep your relationships with them businesslike. If Tellers seem a little cold and matter-of-fact, don't take it personally. They are more concerned with accomplishments and achievements than with relationships. They look for results.

- Encourage and praise Tellers for all the jobs and tasks they get done. But don't overdo the encouragement or they'll be off and running to accomplish more before you finish your statement of appreciation.

Responding to Touchers

- Touchers most appreciate people who are gentle and not brash.

- Touchers do not offer hasty opinions or make quick decisions because they don't want to say anything that might hamper relationships. Help them realize that sharing their thoughts will not negatively affect their relationship with you.

- Touchers ask "Why?" They need information that will explain the reasons why they should do something. Explain to them why they need to put forth the effort on a particular task. Help them see how they will benefit from it and how their participation will help everyone else.

- Touchers have a hard time relaxing in social situations. They don't want to say or do anything that might cause tension among people. Encourage them to understand that a disagreement with someone is not the end of the world. Help them realize that it is possible for people to hold different opinions and still remain friends.

- Touchers do not like to work alone. They need much encouragement and assurance, and they need to feel that they are part of the team. Let them work with you.

- Touchers like to know they are accepted. Take time to show personal interest in them.

- Touchers are hesitant to share their thoughts and ideas. Learn to be patient in communicating with them. Try not to disagree with them in public or when you suspect that a disagreement will hurt their feelings. Otherwise they will close up and not share anything with you.

- To get Touchers to participate, clearly define what you expect from them. Also communicate what you will do to contribute to the relationship or the task at hand.

• Encourage and praise Touchers with warm, personal thanks for their contributions and participation.

Responding to Talkers

• Talkers appreciate people who will listen to them and share with them. Become involved in their interests as much as possible.

• Talkers are intuitive thinkers. They process information and form judgments and opinions quickly. They will also share their opinions openly. Have patience with their quick decisions. They will operate at a feeling level and may not always be able to give you a rational explanation for their behavior.

• Talkers have a tendency to "tell it like it is." Try not to take their comments personally. Many times they are simply letting off steam, and you just happen to be in the way.

• Talkers are relationship oriented, and they want to know who is going to be involved. Encourage a sense of excitement and interaction with people.

- Talkers tend to start many jobs and not complete them. Work with them to accomplish tasks. They like to visit with other people while working. They do not do their best when working alone.

- Talkers tend to exaggerate and overgeneralize. Be alert to and patient with their overstatements.

- Talkers become easily sidetracked. Help them complete the tasks they start. They like to anticipate the future, so help them become excited about what lies ahead.

- Encourage and praise Talkers for their enthusiasm. Publicly recognize them and appreciate them for jobs well done.

Learning Social Styles

Learning to adapt your social style to fit the needs of other social styles is a practical expression of loving our neighbors as ourselves. The great reformer Martin Luther said, "Faith, like light, should always be simple and unbending; while love, like warmth, should beam forth on every side and bend to every necessity of our brethren."

Assignment 1: People Watching

General Behavior	Individual Behavior
Body gestures	Anger or Fear?
Eye contact	Direct or Indirect?
Facial expressions	Facts or Feelings?
How people walk	Fast or Slow?
How they talk	Happy or Sad?
Posture	Loud or Quiet?
Reactions to others	Many or Few?
Response under stress	Outgoing or Restrained?
Speech content	Positive or Negative?
Tone of voice	Rigid or Relaxed?

Assignment 2: Reading People

Thinkers	Tellers
Closed posture	Brisk walk
Eyes look away	Confident posture
Head is rigid	Eyes ahead
Reserved smile	Friendly smile
Tentative walk	Head is up

Touchers	Talkers
Casual walk	Energetic walk
Eyes are unsure	Eyes focused
Gentle smile	Head is relaxed
Head is down	Open posture
Uncertain posture	Responsive smile

Assignment 3: Recognizing People

Thinkers	Tellers
Cautious	Achievers
Detailed	Assertive
Knowledgeable	Discerning
Rational	Insightful
Reserved	Objective

Touchers	Talkers
Compassionate	Charismatic
Considerate	Friendly
Devoted	Optimistic
Supportive	Passionate
Understanding	Visionary

Assignment 4: Relating to People

Thinkers	Tellers
Be calm	Be competent
Be composed	Be efficient
Be deliberate	Be prepared
Be factual	Be punctual
Be reasonable	Be sensible

Touchers	Talkers
Be attentive	Be energetic
Be caring	Be enthusiastic
Be cooperative	Be outgoing
Be helpful	Be relaxed
Be pleasant	Be sociable

Putting It Together in 7 Seconds

1 second: Read

Body Language	Thinker	Teller	Toucher	Talker
Head	Rigid	Up	Down	Relaxed
Eyes	Away	Ahead	Unsure	Focused
Smile	Reserved	Friendly	Gentle	Responsive
Walk	Tentative	Brisk	Casual	Energetic
Posture	Closed	Confident	Uncertain	Open

2-4 seconds: Recognize

	Thinker	Teller	Toucher	Talker
Characteristics	Detailed	Assertive	Supportive	Charismatic
	Reserved	Objective	Compassion	Passionate
	Knowledge-able	Insightful	Considerate	Visionaries
	Cautious	Discerning	Devoted	Friendly
	Rational	Achievers	Understanding	Optimistic
Professions	Scientists	Advisors	Teachers	Sales
	Artists	Consultants	Secretaries	Marketing
	Doctors	Lawyers	Counselors	Business
	Professors	Managers	Healthcare	Entrepreneur
	Engineers	Administrators	Service industry	Public service

5-7 seconds: Relate

	Thinker	Teller	Toucher	Talker
How to Respond	Precise	Professional	Practical	Positive
Remember to Be	Factual	Punctual	Pleasant	Outgoing
	Reasonable	Competent	Attentive	Enthusiastic
	Calm	Prepared	Cooperative	Relaxed
	Deliberate	Efficient	Helpful	Energetic
	Composed	Sensible	Caring	Sociable

Insight

. . . .

You will find as you look back on your life
that the moments when you have
really lived are the moments when you
have done things in the spirit of love.

HENRY DRUMMOND

11

The Shortcut

Scott read and reread the notebook material, but he still had an important question for Gordon. It was time to call him.

"Hi, Gordon. This is Scott. I hope I'm not disturbing you."

"Not at all."

Scott paused to gather his thoughts, and Paddock sensed the slight hesitation.

"I guess we need to meet," said Paddock with a smile in his voice.

"Yes, sir. I could come up to your ranch or we could meet wherever you suggest."

"How about the Starbucks by Sears where you work? I'll be in that area next Tuesday night. How about seven o'clock?"

"That would be great! I sure appreciate your willingness to meet with me. I look forward to our time together."

Scott was excited. He had a burning question that needed an answer and clarification.

When Scott arrived at Starbucks, he bought Gordon's black coffee and an Orange Mocha Frappuccino for himself. He chose a booth in the back corner and hailed Gordon when he arrived.

Gordon came over, shook Scott's hand, and then sat down. "Thanks for the coffee, Scott! I appreciate it."

"No problem," Scott replied.

"So, you have some questions…"

"I have one question that I really need to know the answer to. Obviously, you've been doing this for a long time. You seem to be able to read, recognize, and relate to people almost instantly. How do you do it so quickly? Is there a secret?"

Paddock smiled and leaned back in his chair comfortably.

"It's not often that someone asks me that question. I knew you were smart, but now I know you are also very observant. What I'm about to share with you is not in the notebook. It's only for those very sharp individuals who really want to put these skills into practice."

Scott was listening intently.

"After a number of years of observing people, I developed a shortcut for quickly determining an individual's social style and relating to his or her needs. When I observe or meet someone, I ask myself two questions."

"Now, you've really gotten my interest!"

"As you know, there are four basic social styles: the Thinker, the Teller, the Toucher, and the Talker. To get a quick handle on a particular person's social style, I ask myself two questions. The first one is: 'Are they *up* or *down?*' The second one is: 'Are they *left* or *right?*'"

Paddock noticed the "deer in the headlights" look on Scott's face.

"Stay with me, Scott. Let me illustrate this concept as I talk. That will make it easier to follow." Paddock took out a piece of paper and drew a box. "At the top of the box is the word '*Up.*' Up indicates a person who is 'project oriented.' These people are *task minded.* They are planners, logical, problem solvers, perfectionists, and resourceful individuals.

Project oriented
Up

Down
People oriented

Scott nodded as he took in the information.

"Okay, now I ask whether they are *right* or *left* people." Gordon wrote "Left" on that side of the box. "*Left* indicates discussion-oriented people. They are very team minded. They are thoughtful, helpful, determined, adaptable, and contemplative. Next comes the *right*." He wrote "Right" on the right side of the box. "*Right* indicates decision-oriented people. They are *goal minded.* They come across as confident, commanding, persuasive, forceful, and competent." Gordon drew a large arrow pointing to the "Left" and to the "Right."

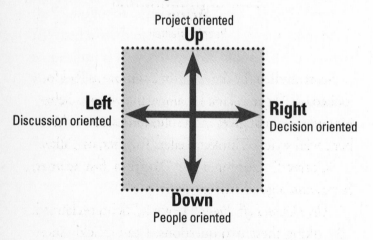

Gordon continued. "If your observations place someone Up and Left, that indicates you're interacting with a Thinker. If you believe someone is Down and Right, that puts him or her into the Talker social style. Likewise, an Up and Right indicates a Teller, and Down and Left indicates a Toucher."

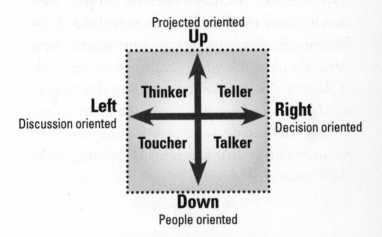

Scott studied the drawing for a minute as Paddock looked on. "I get it. First I evaluate the person's behavior and then that gives me a solid indication of his or her social style—Thinker, Teller, Toucher, or Talker."

"Correct!" Gordon said. "You're a fast learner, Scott, and a good student of people."

"*Up, Down, Left, Right.* I've got it," Scott exclaimed. "By asking these two questions, I can quickly identify a person's style and know the best way to interact with him or her. I see why you call your program 'Seven Seconds to Success'!"

"You will be right in the majority of your encounters with people. This knowledge will help you to meet their needs. As you meet the needs of others, you'll find they will trust you and want to do business with you. Remember, it is simply the Golden Rule of responding to others like you want them to respond to you."

Scott hesitated for a moment. "I need to share something else with you. I finally did it."

"Did what, Scott?"

"I did what you suggested. After I finished reading the book of John, I knew I needed to make a decision. I invited Christ into my heart."

"That's wonderful, Scott!"

"I feel so different now. It's like my whole perspective on life has changed. Even Sarah noticed the change in my attitude. We're now going to church together. Things aren't the same. Is there anything I should do in the area of my spiritual life?"

"When someone invites Jesus to come into his or her life, Scott, God sends his Holy Spirit to dwell within him or her. He will be with you to teach you about God and guide you. He will support you in tough times. I suggest that you read the book of Philippians next. It will be a real encouragement for you."

"I'll be sure to do that."

"It's important to read the Bible every day. May I suggest a very simple, daily Bible study that will help to keep you on track? Select one of the books in the Bible you'd like to read. Read one chapter a day until you are finished with that book. As you read each chapter, take notes. Work on identifying the key verse of the chapter or the central thought. Next, look for God's commands. A command is something to do. Then look for God's promises. A promise is something to be believed. Finally, you might look for personal applications that you received from reading that particular chapter. These are principles or ideas you can apply to your daily life." Gordon could see the excitement in Scott's eyes.

"Thank you so much, Gordon. I only hope I can repay you by teaching others these concepts as well as you have taught them to me."

"I'm sure you will, Scott."

—∿—

Scott's thoughts about the past were suddenly interrupted by the ringing of his cell phone. Without looking at who was calling, he pushed the button and said, "MacFadden Properties. This is Scott. May I help you?"

There was a slight giggle on the other end of the line.

"Why yes. I would like to speak to the president of MacFadden Properties. I'm a very important customer, and I was wondering if Mr. MacFadden would be interested in taking me out to dinner after his open house?"

"Only on one condition."

"What's that?"

"The condition is that you're the most beautiful woman in the world, and your name is Sarah Mac-Fadden."

There was a delightful laugh in response. "How has your day been, honey?"

"It's been a great day. I just met a nice couple from Simi Valley, and I have an offer to deliver on the four bedroom house on Claymore Avenue. On top of that, there are two couples interested in the beach house on Balboa Island in Newport Beach."

"That sounds like a good opportunity for a dinner celebration."

There was a pause and then Scott replied, "You know, Sarah, before you called, I was thinking back to the day when you suggested I meet Gordon Paddock at the book signing at Barnes & Noble. Our lives have really changed since then. I have you to thank for encouraging me to go that day."

"That was a difficult time for us financially, Scott. But look at what has come about! MacFadden Properties has become the third largest real estate agency in Orange County. I'm very proud of you."

"Well, I can't take the credit. I think most of it goes to Gordon, who took the time and interest to help me realize my dreams. I can still hear him quoting the writer Chuck Swindoll: 'We are all faced with a series of great opportunities brilliantly disguised as impossible situations.' I'm now aware that I too have a responsibility to help someone else fulfill his dreams just as Gordon helped me."

Insights

· · · · · · · · · · · · · ·

*The Scriptures teach us the best way of
living, the noblest way of suffering, and the
most comfortable way of dying.*

FLAVEL

———

*One thing I know: The only ones among
you who will really be happy are those who
will have sought and found how to serve.*

ALBERT SCHWEITZER

12

The Questions

Whenever we present the seminars on "7 Seconds to Success," questions arise. Most of them are for clarification and understanding. Some are posed in the form of challenges. Interestingly, the types of questions asked and the way in which they are asked often identify the social style of the individuals asking the questions. Each social style approaches the material from its unique vantage point.

Are the social styles like the signs of the zodiac?

No. Social styles do not depend on positions of the stars or dates of birth to determine or regulate how a person behaves or responds. Social style theory simply seeks to identify habit patterns in individuals' behaviors. The four consistent behavior patterns that continually reappear have been categorized as Thinkers, Tellers, Touchers, and Talkers.

Doesn't the social style system put people in boxes and rob them of their uniqueness and individuality?

Not really. Social styles are kind of like fingerprints. Everyone has fingerprints, and each person's fingerprints are, at the same time, similar to others and distinctly unique. That's the way it is with behavior. Much of human behavior is similar, but at the same time, each person has his or her own unique and individual "behavior print." Social style concepts don't put people in boxes; the system merely identifies the behaviors a person already displays.

How a person responds in a given situation will be similar to how others would respond. The minor variations within a general response will be due to factors of age, education, environment, experience, understanding, social style, and religious upbringing. Understanding social styles doesn't mean we can predict how each individual will respond in every given situation. It does, however, alert us to the *probability* of certain behaviors under certain conditions.

Can social styles be changed?

We personally think it is impossible to change your basic social style. We believe our social styles are intrinsic to our basic, God-given, individual makeup.

There isn't any reason to change your social style. There is no better or best style. Each social style has its own unique and positive contribution to make interpersonal relationships. It would be terribly boring if all of us were the same style. God has made us different from each other—let's enjoy the differences.

Are you sure we can't change our social styles? We behave differently depending on the situation.

Yes, we do act differently at times, depending on a number of factors. We have a "public us" and a "private us," suggesting that we sometimes behave differently when we're alone and when we're with people. When a situation requires it, we can respond more assertively or less assertively than we usually do. We can also change from being task oriented to being relationship oriented or vice versa under certain conditions. But the ability to change temporarily or situationally does not alter our basic styles. It just means we are able to flex and adapt when necessary.

A person can learn to smile on the outside when he is really angry inside. He can help others when he would rather work on his own project. Your job may require you to work with lots of people on a daily basis, and so you do, even though you may not be relationship oriented. You may be very shy, but you have learned to respond differently in social situations where you are required to interact. (Many entertainers adapt in this way.) Your work or community position may require you to speak publicly even though you are not usually outgoing.

We all have the ability to behave differently from our prominent social style when the situation requires it. But when the need for the behavior change is no longer apparent, we will usually drop back into the familiar and comfortable patterns of our basic social style.

Are you saying behavior can't change?

Of course not. Individual behaviors can be changed and modified, but our basic behavior styles of being a Thinker, Teller, Toucher, or Talker will not.

Can the social style concept be misused?

Yes. It has been misused in the past, and it probably will be misused in the future. The social style concept has sometimes been misused in name-calling: "You're a Teller, you run over people"; "You're a Talker, just one big mouth"; "You're a Thinker, who thinks you can never be wrong"; "You're a lazy Toucher only worried about yourself." But people who name-call will do so with any system that's handy. People who put down others usually do it because they are miserable and want others to join them. Sometimes they do it because they are guilty of the same behavior. Others belittle people because they want to elevate themselves.

Social styles are misused when they become an excuse for negative behavior. Someone may say, "I know I was a little harsh, but I'm a Teller," as if his or her social style included the right to hurt others. It doesn't.

Social styles are misused when someone endeavors to employ the information to manipulate others for selfish means. For example, a salesperson may say, "If I tell lots of emotional stories to this Talker customer, I'll make a sale." Building bridges works better than building barriers.

Social styles are also misused when they become a tool for determining or judging motives instead of behavior. For example, "She is such a perfectionist. She just wants to be judge and jury all wrapped into one." Another example is, "He pretends to be a diplomat, but he's just an apple polisher." The social style system helps us identify, classify, and predict the future behavior of ourselves and others, but it is not a measuring stick for motives.

Isn't the social style program similar to other programs?

The social style system first adapted by David W. Merrill and Roger H. Reid is not new. The basic ideas have been around for centuries, dating back to Hippocrates (460–370 b.c.). The "System Comparison" chart on the next page reveals the variety of terms that have been used to describe the same four basic social styles.

System Comparison

System & Proponents	High Relationship; More Talk	High Task; More Talk	High Task; More Ask	High Relationship; More Ask
Four Temperament Theory (Hippocrates, O. Hallesby, LaHaye)	Sanguine	Choleric	Melancholy	Phlegmatic
Jay Hall	Synergistic	Win–lose	Yield–lose	Lose–leave
William Marston	Inducement of others	Dominance	Steadiness	Compliance
Donald T. Simpson	Integration	Power	Suppression	Denial
Stuart Atkins	Adapting–dealing	Controlling–talking	Supporting–giving	Conserving–holding
Bill Sloan	Feelers	Sensors	Intuitors	Thinkers
Adickies	Dogmatic	Agnostic	Innovative	Traditional
Thomas–Kilmann	Collaborating	Competing	Accommodating	Avoiding
Robert E. Lefton	Dominant–warm	Dominant–hostile	Submissive–hostile	Submisssive–warm
Theodore Levitt	Perceptive Thinkers	Intuitive Thinkers	Systematic Thinkers	Receptive Thinkers
Spranger	Artistic	Theoretic	Religious	Economic
Keirsey–Bates	Dionysian	Promethean	Epimethean	Apollonian
Myers–Briggs	Perceptive types	Intuitive types	Sensing types	Judging types
David Kolb	Accommodator	Converger	Assimilator	Diverger
Kahler	Rebel	Workaholic	Dreamer	Reactor
David W. Merrill Robert H. Reid / Bob Phillips and Kimberly Alyn	Expressive	Driver	Analytical	Amiable
Gary Coffey and Bob Phillips	Talker	Teller	Thinker	Toucher

Can social styles be observed in children?

Without question. It is fairly easy to identify children who are more assertive and those who are less assertive. You can go to any grade school and observe this. Some children are task oriented and others are relationship oriented. Even in babies we can see major differences in behavior. Thinker and Toucher babies are often very easygoing, quiet, and cuddly. On the other hand, Teller and Talker babies are often restless, loud, and very active.

Can children understand social style concepts?

Yes, they can. In fact, children understand the actions and behaviors of others before they understand the meanings of words. They know which of their relatives are loud and talkative, and which ones are quiet. They sense those who are very friendly and those who are reserved or introverted.

As children begin school, they use different words to describe the social styles of their classmates. They might identify the Thinker child as a "bookworm." The might see the Teller child as a "bully." The Toucher child might be described as the "teacher's pet." The Talker child might be known as the "class clown." The terms vary, but the behaviors do not. When social styles material is shared with children, they grasp the concepts quickly and learn the terms easily.

Social Styles—
Likes and Dislikes Summaries

The Thinkers

What They Value	What Annoys Them
Accuracy	Aggressiveness
Competence	Change
Critical thinking	Clamor
Details	Clutter
Efficiency	Disorganization
Facts	Evasiveness
Logic	Exaggeration
Organization	Hastiness
Quality	Inaccuracy
Rules and regulations	Inadequacy
Security	Incompetence
Stability	Invasiveness
Structure	Mediocrity
Tradition	Shouting

The Tellers

What They Value	What Annoys Them
Achievement	Boredom
Challenge	Dependency
Competition	Details
Control	Excuses
Debates	Hypersensitivity
Decisiveness	Indecisiveness
Goals	Irresponsibility
Independence	Laziness
Leadership	Lethargy
Power	Over-analyzing
Productivity	Over-emotional
Responsibility	Procrastination
Speed	Small talk
Success	Taking orders

The Touchers

What They Value	What Annoys Them
Approval	Conflict
Benevolence	Controversy
Coaching	Discourteousness
Cohesiveness	Disharmony
Comfort	Disrespect
Compassion	Harshness
Contribution	Impatience
Cooperation	Insensitivity
Friendliness	Pressure
Kindness	Pushiness
Loyalty	Rudeness
Peacefulness	Rushing
Relationships	Tension
Trust	Yelling

The Talkers

What They Value	What Annoys Them
Adventure	Boredom
Change	Details
Creativity	Formality
Enthusiasm	Ritual
Excitement	Routine
Flexibility	Rules
Freedom	Schedules
Innovation	Slowness
Spontaneity	Stagnation
Uniqueness	Structure
Unpredictability	Tedium
Versatility	Uncreative
Vision	Unoriginal

Recommended Reading

For additional and expanded information on social styles and conflict resolution we recommend these books.

Alessandra, Anthony J., PhD, Phillip S. Wexler, and Rick Barbera. *Non-Manipulative Selling.* New York: Touchstone/Simon & Schuster, 1992, ebook 2009.

LaHaye, Tim. *Transformed Temperaments.* Carol Stream, IL: Tyndale House Publishers, 1993.

Nierenberg, Gerard I., Henry H. Calero, and Gabriel Grayson. *How to Read a Person Like a Book.* Garden City Park, NY: Square One Publishers, 2009.

Phillips, Bob, and Kimberly Alyn. *How to Deal with Annoying People.* Eugene, OR: Harvest House Publishers, 2011.

Merrill, David W., and Roger H. Reid. *Personal Styles and Effective Performance.* Philadelphia: Chilton Book Company, 1981.

Scheflen, Albert E. *Body Language and Social Order.* New York: Prentice-Hall, 1972.

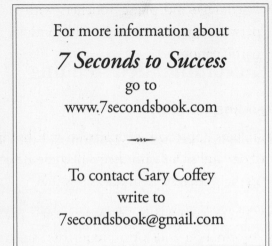

For more information about

7 Seconds to Success

go to

www.7secondsbook.com

———~~~———

To contact Gary Coffey

write to

7secondsbook@gmail.com

———~~~———

More Harvest House Books
by Bob Phillips

The Awesome Book of Bible Trivia

Controlling Your Emotions Before They Control You

How Can I Be Sure?

How to Deal with Annoying People

Men Are Slobs, Women Are Neat

Overcoming Anxiety and Depression